READ ALL ABOUT IT!

W
FRANKLIN WATTS
LONDON·SYDNEY

This edition 2004

First published in 2001 by Franklin Watts
96 Leonard Street, LONDON EC2A 4XD

Franklin Watts Australia
45-51Huntley Street,
Alexandria, NSW 2015

Copyright © Franklin Watts 2001 and 2004

Series editor: Rachel Cooke
Assistant editors: Adrian Cole and Kate Newport
Designer: John Christopher, White Design
Picture researcher: Sue Mennell

A CIP catalogue record for this book is available from
the British Library.

ISBN 0 7496 5678 6

Dewey Classification 362.29

Printed in Malaysia

Acknowledgements:

Cartoons Andy Hammond pp. 12, 16, 21; Sholto Walker p. 20.
Photographs Front cover: Franklin Watts tr; Topham
Picturepoint, ca; Rex Features (Gordon Jack), cb;
Popperfoto (MonteFresco/PPP) br; PYMCA (Rob Watkins),
bl; Back cover: PYMCA (Rob Watkins); Inside: Advertising
Archives p. 22; Cephas p. 9b (Emma Bourg); Norman
Clayton p. 27; Pam Dunsford/Chapel Hill Winery (c/o
Australian Wine Agencies, London) p. 19; Format pp. 14b
(Paula Solloway), 16 (Mo Wilson); Ronald Grant Archive p.
23 (courtesy of Granada); © Guinness Limited p. 22;
Photofusion pp. 6t (Paul Baldesare), 15t (Paul Baldesare);
Popperfoto pp. 5t (Reuters), 28 (Monte Fresco/PPP);
Portman Group p. 3b; PYMCA pp. 25 (Rob Watkins); Rex
Features pp. 3tc (Paul Brown), 8 (Sipa/Anatoli Iolis), 9t
(Sipa/Tourneret), 12, 13 (Richard Young), 14t (Sipa), 15b
(Paul Brown), 18, 24t (Gordon Jack), 24b (Erik Pendzich);
Topham Picturepoint pp. 3tl, 3tr (John Sitwell), 4, 5b (Fiona
Hanson), 7 (David Giles), 10, 17 (Michael Stepens), 29 (John
Sitwell); Franklin Watts pp. 6b, 26; Wellcome Trust Photo
Library p. 11.

EDITOR'S NOTE

Read All About It: Alcohol takes the form of a newspaper called *The Alcohol News*. In it you can find a lot of articles about different subjects and many facts. It also includes opinions about these facts, sometimes obviously as in the editorial pages, but sometimes more subtly in a news article: for example in the article concerning pub closures (page 7). Like any newspaper, you must ask yourself when you read the book 'What does the writer think?' and 'What does the writer want me to think?', as well as 'What do I think?'.

However, there are several ways in which *The Alcohol News* is not and cannot be a newspaper. It deals with one issue rather than many and it has not been published on a particular day at a particular moment in history, with another version to be published tomorrow. While *The Alcohol News* aims to look at the major issues concerning alcohol, the events reported have not necessarily taken place in the past few days but rather over the past few years. They have been included because they raise questions that are relevant to the issue today and that will continue to be so in the future.

Another important difference is that *The Alcohol News* has been written by one person, not many, in collaboration with an editor. They have used different 'voices' and, in some instances, such as the letters and the discussion column, pseudonyms. However, the people and events reported and commented on are real.

There are plenty of other things in *The Alcohol News* that are different from a true newspaper. Try looking at the book alongside a real newspaper and think about, not only where we have got the approach right, but where we have got it wrong! Finally, we would like to thank Bindi Singh Sohi and Norman Clayton for their contributions to page 27. Enjoy reading *The Alcohol News*.

THE ALCOHOL NEWS

THREE BILLION BOOZE BINGE

The News Editor

Alcohol consumption is costing us a staggering £3.3 billion – and that's not in bar bills! Leading pressure group Alcohol Concern have put this price tag on the costs taxpayers have to meet as a result of drink-related accidents, NHS bills and crime.

In the past politicians have sought to reduce this figure by raising tax on alcohol sales. However, despite this move, hospital beds, prisons and police cells continue to fill with the victims of excessive drinking. With 40% of men between 16-24 drinking more than the recommended daily allowance (RDA) of 3-4 units in one session, and 20% of women drinking more than 2-3 units, the government is under mounting pressure to find alternative approaches.

One suggestion, outlined in the government's White Paper on licensing reform, has been to extend the opening hours of licensed premises to 24 hours. This move, which is common practice in the rest of Europe, is intended to reduce what is seen by many as the main cause of anti-social behaviour – binge-drinking.

However, these plans are not universally welcomed. An Institute of Alcohol Studies survey found that 59% of those questioned opposed extending opening hours. ■

Leaflets help promote Prove it! scheme.

400,000 TEENAGERS PROVE IT

The voluntary scheme, 'Prove It!', where a proof of age card helps those over 18 prove that they are legally entitled to buy alcohol, has been hailed as a great success. Developed by the Portman Group, the drinks industry's self-regulatory body, the card costs just five pounds to register and has attracted 400,000 applicants. It is popular with licensees as it gives greater confidence when selling to younger-looking drinkers. However, the BMA says it is not enough.

FOR THE BMA'S VIEW: SEE PAGE 7

WHAT SHALL WE DO WITH THE DRUNKEN SAILOR?

New proposals to cut down on drink-related accidents at sea may take the fizz out of pleasure boat holidays

Fifty-one young party-goers died when the Marchioness sank in 1989.

Home Affairs Editor

The government is set to tackle alcohol abuse afloat after a series of alcohol-related accidents (see box).

The difficulty for law enforcement agencies, however, will be to find a rule which prevents professional ship crews from being 'drunk in charge' of a vessel. In turn, this must operate without also applying to private leisure craft.

A NIP OF RUM

Boating for pleasure is big business around Britain's coasts, and in many inland waterways such as canals and the Norfolk Broads. A 'nip of rum' is considered by many a vital part of the experience and so tougher regulations would be highly unpopular.

The Institute of Alcohol Studies, in an early response to the Home Office consultation, points out that enforcing alcohol limits on holidaymakers will prove extremely hard for police forces.

Beyond the resources needed to provide adequate patrols on waterways, legally it would be tricky to identify who is responsible for a vessel when more than one person is on board. ■

ACCIDENT AHOY:

■ The Marchioness river boat tragedy on the Thames, in 1989, claimed the lives of 51 party-goers and crew when a dredger, the Bowbelle, collided with the pleasure-cruiser. The inquest into the accident concluded with a proposal to regulate drinking aboard ship.

■ A tribunal has heard that a skipper of a 50,000-tonne oil tanker and three crewmen had to be rescued by RAF helicopter when returning to their ship in a dinghy after a pub crawl in Aberdeen. Witnesses at the MacDuff Arms reported that the men had consumed 'roughly' seven pints of beer each. The captain was found guilty of breaching a strict 'no alcohol' company policy, for which tanker-owners Mobil sacked him, but found no cause to remove his mariner's licence.

■ The Marine Accident Investigation Agency recorded the deaths of two fishermen as linked to excessive alcohol consumption. The men fell into the dock while returning to their vessel after drinking ashore. They fell as they were crossing from one boat to another. ■

DNA BLAMED FOR DRUNKENNESS: SEE PAGE 14

UK Soft on Drink-Driving

The News Editor

A senior European official has called on Britain to bring rules on drink-driving in line with European laws.

Vice-President of the European Commission, Loyola de Palacio del Valle-Lersundi, has asked Britain, Finland, Ireland, Luxembourg and Italy to bring legal blood-alcohol limits for drivers down to the EU-recommended 0.5 grams per litre.

NO LOWER LIMIT

The Labour government had pledged to lower the British limit from 0.8g% to 0.5g% in its 1997 election manifesto. However, the promise has not as yet been fulfilled. This is perhaps a surprising decision given that the police, virtually the whole road safety community and public opinion are in favour of imposing the lower limit. Even the Department of Transport's own figures estimate that around 50 lives could be saved each year with the 0.5%g limit.

Miss de Palacio drew attention to the higher legal limit in Britain after figures were released showing that 42,553 people died in road accidents in Europe in 1998. A significant percentage of these deaths were due to drunk drivers. ■

DIANA INQUIRY
— DEATHS DUE TO DRUNK DRIVER

The French courts have concluded that the death of Princess Diana, in a car accident in 1997, was due to drink-driving.

Judge Hervé Stéphane found that the driver of Diana's car, Henri Paul, was not fit to drive, owing to a combination of alcohol and anti-depressant pills.

The judge's report was also critical of Diana's companion Dodi Fayed, who died alongside her. It notes that it was Mr Fayed's decision to order Henri Paul, who was off-duty and had been drinking, to chauffeur the pair away from the Ritz Hotel, Paris.

Mohamed al-Fayed, Dodi Fayed's father and the owner of the Ritz, Paris, announced he would appeal against the ruling. ■

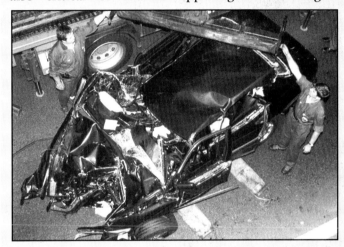

The wreckage of the Fayeds' crashed Mercedes being cleared away.

Not everyone needs a reminder about drink driving.

Shock tactics have proven vital in the battle against drink-driving.

The UK has the best record in the world for reducing drink-driving offences. However, a recent MORI survey found that 7 out of 10 people still feel that it is a major social problem. Anti drink-drive advertising campaigns, which have included *Drinking and Driving Wrecks Lives* and *Think!*, have undoubtedly contributed to this reduction. Britain has seen the total number of casualties in drink-drive accidents fall from 23,390 in 1984 to around 16,000 in 1995

Drinkers advised to stop at five units

Timing, Gentlemen, Please

Unit allowance – don't spend it all at once.

Government guidelines about safe alcohol consumption are being misused by consumers, a new report suggests.

The study by Datamonitor compared alcohol use across several European countries.

According to Richard Robinson, Datamonitor's Drinks Industry analyst, consumers in Britain are treating the weekly 'allowance' of units for men and women like a bank account.

'Many consumers are using a "debits and credits" system,' says Robinson. He added: 'Consumers feel one session of "being good", such as going to the gym, earns them an indulgence such as an alcoholic drink.'

The most important problem emerging from the statistics is that some consumers exhaust their entire 'allowance' in one session. This so-called 'binge-drinking' – anything over five units of alcohol – is extremely stressful for the body.

One solution might be if government guidelines concentrate on daily, not weekly allowances.

Alcohol campaigners also want government education programmes to stress that a 'night off' the booze does not give anyone licence to drink to excess the following day. ■

WEEKLY UNIT ALLOWANCE

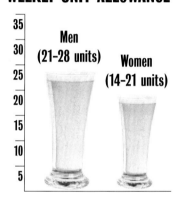

Men (21-28 units)

Women (14-21 units)

1 unit of alcohol = 1/2 pint of average strength lager, beer or cider (3.5% Alcohol By Volume); 25ml measure of spirit (40% ABV); small glass of wine (9% ABV).

ALL IN A LATHER

The days of being cheated out of a full pint may soon be at an end. The Government has asked the Campaign for Real Ale (CAMRA) to assist in finding a solution to the age-old phenomenon of the under-filled pint glass.

By law, beer that is sold in pint glasses must be poured up to the level of a printed line on the glass, which marks where a full measure should be. Some pint glasses have no lines but these are meant for use with drinks that do not produce a 'head'.

The problem arises when beers with frothy heads are served in glasses without lines. This allows landlords to squeeze up to 76 'pints' out of a 72-pint keg of beer, by including the head as part of the pint. Estimates suggest that the consumer ends up paying almost £160 million each year on the missing beer.

The pub trade already has a voluntary code of conduct which states that a pint should be 95% liquid and it is suggesting this should become law. But CAMRA's Head of Campaigns, Mike Benner, feels a figure of 97% or 98% would be fairer to the consumer.

UPHILL STRUGGLE

A previous attempt to bring the British pint up to full measure was sabotaged by MPs sympathetic to the pub trade in 1998. This attempt faces a similar uphill struggle. Brewers are already suggesting that if the correct measure is made law, they will retaliate by putting up prices. ■

Save Our Pubs!

A new initiative aims to halt the decline of the traditional village pub

With statistics showing an average of 20 pubs closing per month across Britain, the Campaign for Real Ale (CAMRA) and the Countryside Agency have teamed up to try to halt the decline.

Part of the problem lies in falling demand, but CAMRA is very concerned that some publicans are deliberately making their pubs unprofitable in order to win permission to sell them as homes – making a fast buck at the community's expense.

According to the Countryside Agency's Tony Dadoun, 'The public house is the focal point of the rural community.' Together with CAMRA, the agency has produced a booklet informing publicans of the ways they can diversify their services which, it is hoped, will give them the best chance of survival.

A CHANGE OF USE

To combat 'deliberate failure', the campaign has issued council planning officers across Britain – who have to approve the change of use from a public house to a private dwelling – with a Public House Viability Test.

The test is designed to help officials tell the difference between pubs in real difficulty, and those which are made deliberately unprofitable in order to justify a change of use.

CAMRA's Mike Benner said: 'The loss of the local pub is a disaster for village communities and our test aims to bring some consistency to planning processes across the country.' CAMRA is also urging government to ease the tax burden on pubs, as it already does for local post offices and village halls, making them more competitive. ■

Public house or private flats? Is the rural pub on its last legs?

BMA URGES TOUGHER REGULATION

The British Medical Association (BMA) has condemned the existing arrangements for regulation of the drinks industry. In its report, *Alcohol and Young People*, the association strongly recommends that the government set up an independent over-seer in place of the industry's preferred self-regulatory body, the Portman Group.

Sir William Asscher, of the BMA's board of science and education, found that the existing controls were failing to protect young people. He said: 'Part of the solution lies in health education, but teenagers, with their delusions of immortality, are notoriously difficult to influence.' The report suggests concerted action by the government, including:

■ Test purchasing – sending children to buy alcohol to test whether retailers are fulfilling the responsibilities of their licence and refusing to sell to under-18s

■ Training – to ensure that landlords and off-licence staff are aware of their legal obligations

■ Health Warnings – clear health warnings, as provided for tobacco, on all packaging and advertising.

IS THERE A FUTURE FOR THE SOAP PUB? FIND OUT ON PAGE 23

RED OR DEAD?

The opening up of the ex-Soviet states has resulted in an astonishing growth in alcohol abuse and associated health problems.

International Editor

Russians have long been famous for their love of vodka and for their heavy drinking. Mikhail Gorbachev, the Soviet president who initiated Perestroika, or 'reconstruction' of the Russian nation, was the only leader in living memory to have tackled the alcoholism problem head-on. He destroyed unlicensed alcohol production, imprisoned bootleggers, raised the price of vodka and arrested people for public drunkenness.

His solutions might have been extreme, but Russians may soon look back on his strict attitude with some nostalgia. Deaths due to alcohol were reduced to a mere 176 per 100,000 citizens, saving an estimated 600,000 lives over three years.

With the opening up of Russian society, Gorbachev's approach was abandoned, and alcohol consumption rose more than five times. Vodka can now be bought for less than a pound per litre. The alcohol-related death rate has soared to record levels, about 500 deaths per 100,000 people, or six times the rate in European countries.

DRAMATIC SWING

A study by the British medical journal, *The Lancet*, finds that life expectancy trends are closely related to this unusually dramatic swing in alcohol consumption. Life expectancy in Russia is now a mere 57 years, six years less than at the beginning of the 1990s.

Will Russians look back with regret to the days when they had to do what they were told? Or do they have to bear this increased loss of life as an inevitable price of freedom? ■

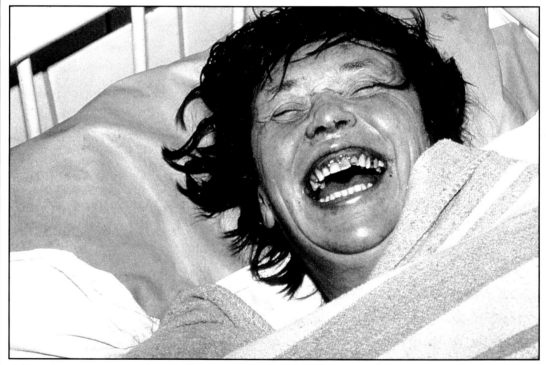

A Russian woman in hospital appears to see the funny side of her alcohol problem.

'Moonshine' deaths in El Salvador

Up to 120 people have died, and several have been blinded, after a spirit containing industrial alcohol went on sale in the San Vincente province of El Salvador.

Methanol, better known for its properties as an anti-freeze, appears to have been added to the drink to give it more 'kick'. But this form of alcohol is highly toxic.

The El Salvadorean government has banned sales of spirit alcohol for 10 days in an attempt to limit the crisis. Two arrests have been made, and industrial users of methanol are being asked to account for their stocks, to ensure that no further poisonous 'brews' can be produced. ■

In Nairobi, Kenya, police reported 75 hospitalisations after slum-dwellers drank a local moonshine, chang'aa, that had been reinforced with raw ethanol, another more toxic form of alcohol. Up to 20 regulars at an illegal drinking den, or 'shebeen', are thought to have died, and several more were blinded. ■

Cannabis Safer than Booze

A Canadian research team has blown the whistle on a suppressed World Health Organisation (WHO) report, in which alcohol is found to be more dangerous than cannabis.

The Addiction Research Foundation (ARF), based in Toronto's Centre for Addiction and Mental Health, alerted the science journal *New Scientist* to the WHO's embarrassed silence on the issue.

EMBARRASSED

The WHO report, *Cannabis: A Health Perspective*, included only summary information. However, the research papers behind the report have now been published in full by ARF as *The Health Effects of Cannabis*.

The WHO explained its omission of the controversial parts of the document by casting doubt on the 'reliability and public health significance of such comparisons'.

This impressed neither the authors, who sought a balanced attitude, nor the *New Scientist*, which concluded: 'In most of the comparisons [the report] makes between cannabis and alcohol, the illegal drug comes out better – or at least on a par – with the legal one.'

The authors use a global health measure known as Disability-Adjusted Life-Years. DALYs lost around the world through illness and injury include 3.5% directly due to alcohol, 2.6% to tobacco, and 0.6% due to all illegal drugs. ■

Is this lawbreaker more responsible than a wine-lover?

A wage in wine has cost South Africa's workers dear.

SOUTH AFRICA DROPS THE 'DOP'

B lack workers in South Africa's wine-growing regions are suffering the after-effects of a barbarous apartheid tradition known as the 'dop'.

Foreign Affairs Editor

Before apartheid fell with the election of the African National Congress party in 1994, white vineyard owners routinely issued their black workers with a bottle and a half of wine. The resultant alcohol addiction allowed them to get away with extremely low wages.

With the end of apartheid, the practice became illegal. However, the after-effects are in many ways worse. Alcoholic workers now spend their meagre wages on the drink that was formerly free, and risk their lives in illegal, violent drinking dens. ■

The Red Wine Effect

A regular swig of red wine may keep this French peasant's heart healthy – but what is it doing to his liver?

The US Health Department has stated that alcohol may be good for you. Buried in a report the Department finished in January 1996 lurks the phrase 'Moderate drinking may lower the risk of heart attacks.'

The Health Editor

The finding comes long after everyone else in the medical community had recognised that France, one of the world's heaviest-drinking nations, suffers relatively fewer heart attacks per head than similar developed countries.

In fact, only Japan has a lower heart attack rate – and the Japanese eat hardly any dairy products compared with the tonnes of cheese consumed in France.

A HEALTH TONIC

There are various explanations for this odd dietary fact. Most opinions focus on the role of the non-alcoholic components of red wine, including Phenol and antioxidants. However, it is not necessary to drink wine to obtain these. In fact a study, published in the *American Journal of Clinical Nutrition*, has found that beneficial effects of certain wine ingredients persist longer in the blood if no alcohol is consumed. As a result, health food stores already sell powdered, non-alcoholic red wine extracts as a health tonic.

Another health fact from France should give US health officials – and red wine drinkers – pause for thought. Alcohol use may relax the heart, but it places major chemical strains on the liver. The French record on liver disease runs at almost double that of its Western neighbours. ■

BEER GOOD FOR BREAST CANCER?

Jaak Janssens of the Limburg University Centre, Belgium, has found evidence that a fall in the consumption of traditional Belgian 'table beer' (around 1.1% alcohol), in favour of modern sugary drinks, could provide a key to a rise in breast cancer. Insulin affects many of the hormones involved in the development of the breast. Irregular insulin 'spikes', such as those caused by soft drinks, might create lesions in breast cells, giving rise to cancer later in life.

Pregnancy Controversy

A new helpline for pregnant women has sparked a row over Foetal Alcohol Syndrome.

The helpline, launched by a Scottish group, aims to alert women to the risks involved in drinking whilst pregnant.

Foetal Alcohol Syndrome induces brain disorders and physical disabilities in a small number of children each year, but the figures and causes are in dispute.

Helpline co-ordinator Jane Murphy is anxious to warn mothers that the condition can be caused by very low levels of alcohol consumption during pregnancy. She has also claimed that up to 140 children are born with impairments each week in the UK as a result of their mothers' alcohol use during pregnancy.

But other experts are not convinced that mothers will benefit from such advice. Cath Cakebread of the Scottish Council on Alcohol regrets the additional stress expectant mothers face after such advice: 'It worries me that women are not enjoying their pregnancies as they should because of the stress and the uncertainty.'

HIDDEN DANGERS

Medical practitioners are also wary of scaring mothers off small amounts of alcohol. Children born to women with severe drink problems are often healthy, suggesting that there is another factor involved which has yet to be identified. A further problem is that the number of full-blown FAS cases recorded each year in the UK is so small that it is difficult to make scientific sense of the causes involved. ■

Should pregnant drinkers be scared?

Side-Effects Cause Storm

American research into the drug Ondansetron, used to treat cancer patients for nausea, has thrown up an interesting side-effect. Patients given the drug cut their alcohol use by up to 50%. Dr Bankole Johnson of Texas University's Health Science Center hopes the drug can be used to help people suffering from long-term alcohol dependency. ■

Student STD Hot-Spot

Trent NHS Region, based around Nottingham, reports double the national average figure for sexually transmitted diseases in Britain. Dr Richard Slack of the Nottingham Health Authority puts the anomaly down to Nottingham's vibrant student community and nightlife. 'Alcohol often means people may not be as careful as they should be,' he notes. ■

Death Rate Rises

Leading pressure group Alcohol Concern has drawn attention to a worrying rise in the rate of deaths linked to alcohol. According to their research, alcohol-related deaths recorded by hospitals in Britain rose from 3,000 per year in the late 1980s to over 5,000 per year by 1997. Subsequent statistics, which are still being analysed, suggest this trend is continuing upwards. ■

Hairy Dog Stories

Alcohol comes in all colours, strengths and flavours, but they all seem to have one thing in common: the morning after.

Modern science has been reluctant to invest resources in investigating the dreaded hangover. Perhaps an anti-hangover pill would simply encourage life-threatening drinking behaviour. Hangovers are also extremely complex. Symptoms are caused by a vast number of different biological and chemical processes happening all at once.

So those who over-indulge in drink have to turn to old wives' tales for a cure. But what do they have going for them?

■ **Hair of the dog** The best known hangover cure, 'hair of the dog', is not actually a cure at all! The saying goes that you should take a smaller dose of what caused the problem to start with, 'the hair of the dog that bit you'. Of course, this is just another glass of alcohol, most popular of which is vodka with tomato juice. The reason it

IF HE REALLY DID HAVE THE 'HAIR OF THE DOG', I'D BE BALD BY NOW!

seems to work is simple. Your body prioritises tackling alcohol, a serious poison. By the time your hangover strikes the morning after, part of the pain and lethargy you feel is because your body is working on the lesser poisons into which it has converted the alcohol overnight. As soon as you add more alcohol to the system, the body drops this work and goes back to processing the alcohol. Great! Trouble being, as soon as this alcohol is processed there's even more pain in store!

■ **Greasy fry-ups** Tradition has it that a Great British fried breakfast is the perfect hangover cure, especially if eaten before bed. Science agrees – to some extent – at least as far as eggs are concerned. They contain cysteine, an amino acid used by the liver to break down toxins. Drawbacks? This only helps with one aspect of the hangover. It can

Mmm! Just what the doctor ordered.

also be a bit hard to face a smelly plate of steaming greasy food when you are hung over. Your body is on full alert against consuming any new poisons, and the slightest hint of a taste or smell of food threatens to trigger the body's last line of defence, the emetic reflex (throwing up). Plain toast and unsugared cereal are better than nothing.

■ **Water before bedtime** A pint or two of water drunk before bedtime can help prevent dehydration. Alcohol inhibits your kidneys' capacity to recycle fluids, causing you to urinate more fluid than is strictly healthy. This results in dehydration, causing symptoms from a dry mouth to a headache as your brain temporarily shrinks! Drinking water seems to help some people more than others, for unknown reasons.

■ **Light exercise** The last thing you feel like doing under a hangover is strenuous activity. But part of the sluggishness you feel the morning after is due to the lactic acid that has built up in your muscles, while your body concentrates on processing alcohol. Light exercise stimulates your liver into returning to processing lactic acid.

■ **Not mixing your drinks** There are many expressions suggesting that sticking to one drink all evening helps prevent hangovers. The most famous in English is probably 'Never mix Grape and Grain', i.e. avoid mixing grain-based drinks, such as beers and certain spirits, with wines and fortified wine drinks such as sherry. Science agrees, up to a point. Each type of drink carries its own unique varieties of poisons, each of which may contribute to a hangover. By sticking to one drink, you limit the number of different 'inputs' to the hangover experience. The more different types of alcohol you consume, the greater the number of different kinds of aches you will experience the next day.

■ **Don't drink!** In the end, a hangover is your body's way of suggesting that you stop poisoning yourself. Like certain illegal drugs, the after-effects are best thought of as the inevitable withdrawal symptoms. Drinking in moderation, or not at all, is the only guaranteed solution. ■

'Men have been getting drunk for years, so why should I suddenly stop? In fact, I've got more catching up to do!'

'My day is so stressful I like nothing more than to unwind with friends in a club or bar. A glass of wine or two helps me to relax and take things a bit easier.'

Changing habits among young women are creating new health risks.

WINE, WOMEN AND WONGA

Despite recent efforts by government ministers and health experts, young women are drinking more than they were five years ago.

A report by industrial research experts Datamonitor found that British women aged 18-24 were likely to consume around 203 litres of alcoholic drink per year. The figure recorded for the same group back in 1999 was 172 litres per year - already higher than health officials would like.

Datamonitor found that UK women were the heaviest female drinkers in the European countries they studied, consuming almost four times as much

as their Italian sisters, and three times as much as French women.

The industry experts predict that this sector will continue to grow across Europe, as young women become financially independent, as attitudes to female drunkenness change, and as drinking venues become more welcoming to women.

The woman-friendly bar typically has large windows at the front, and a light airy atmosphere. Datamonitor believes that women drinkers like to have food available, and expect to choose from a range of wines and 'FABs' - Flavoured Alcoholic Beverages. ■

DNA Makes You Drunk

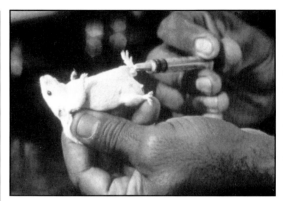

Scientists have bred alcoholic mice to study the effects of drinking.

Alcoholism is a significant social problem in most countries, particularly in the West. But is there a genetic explanation for why people become dependent on drink?

Before researchers could address this question they had to find suitable test subjects. Normal laboratory animals, including mice and monkeys, naturally avoided the toxic qualities of alcoholic substances.

Then a team, led by Drs McClearn and Rodgers at the University of California, Berkeley, made an astonishing breakthrough. By careful selective breeding, they created a new strain of laboratory mouse which loved the poisonous substance.

ALCOHOLIC MOUSE

Mouse strain C57BL/Crgl happily lapped up quantities of alcohol whenever it was provided. This development enables scientists to use the engineered mouse to improve our understanding of alcohol's effects under laboratory conditions, but also raises an important question for alcohol treatment: does the alcoholic mouse prove that alcoholism is an inherited disease?

Studies of human drinkers have shown that, while around 0.1% of women as a whole are clinically dependent on alcohol, 10% of female relatives of alcoholics are afflicted.

For some these statistics suggest genes are at work and there is a hereditary element to alcoholism. However, others point to social factors: genetically-related people are more likely to belong to the same socio-economic group. If one family member is an alcoholic, this suggests that other family members are more likely to abuse alcohol. It is also an indicator of social deprivation. Alcoholism among the poorest 20% of Britons occurs at twice the rate of that among the richest 20%.

Even within the terms of genetic science, it seems hard to explain why humans are the only mammals we know of (apart from C57BL/Crgl) with a liking for alcohol. And what benefits to survival, reproduction or health would such a 'gene' offer?

Another criticism of the genetic explanation points out that addiction is itself not a clear scientific category.

The object of the obsession seems to be of less importance than the desire to repeat a behaviour over and over again, like shopping or eating chocolate. More DNA testing is likely before any firm conclusions can be drawn. ■

Do families pass down alcohol habits through DNA or through their behaviour?

Kids Aren't All Right

New research suggests that alcohol awareness is failing to prevent young people from abusing alcohol.

The figures, published in Alcohol Concern's report *Britain's Ruin*, are taken from attitude surveys and hospital admissions records from the Royal Liverpool Children's Hospital.

The hospital figures show a 1,000% increase in admissions of 9-16-year-olds due to alcohol abuse, between the years 1985 and 1996.

Patients included in the study were either resuscitated from alcohol overdoses, or treated for injuries sustained as a result of drunken accidents and violent assaults.

Attitude surveys conducted on behalf of Alcohol Concern also show worrying secondary risks arising from alcohol abuse. In particular, the campaign group discovered that one in seven 16-24-year-olds reported having unprotected sex while drunk. Pregnancy and sexually transmitted diseases had not been taken into account in previous surveys of the harm caused to young drinkers.

Alcohol Concern concludes that so-called 'alcopop' drinks are a significant contributor to young people's early abuse of alcohol, and urges stronger measures against drinks manufacturers targeting the youth market. ■

DO YOU BLAME THE ADVERTISERS? TURN TO PAGE 22

DO YOU BLAME THE ADVERTISERS? TURN TO PAGE 22

BOTTOM OF THE POPS

Alcopops, drinks in colourful bottles with a sweet taste masking their alcohol content, continue to pose problems for alcohol educators.

Though there is no sign of an increase in the numbers of 11-15-year-olds consuming alcohol over the last ten years, government statistics show that teenagers who do drink are consuming ever-larger amounts in 'binge-drinking' sessions. The drinks industry watchdog, the Portman Group, has recently upheld complaints made separately against four alcoholic drinks: 'Sorted', 'Zulu 42', 'Wild Brew' and 'Cannabis'. They were found, largely for reasons of label design and product name, to be in breach of the industry's Code of Practice. Group director, Jean Coussins, said: 'The sanctions deployed by the Code and the widespread support from retailers, ensure that products which breach the Code do disappear from the market.' However, this self-regulation has not stopped fierce competition within the drinks industry to win the youth market. As a result, researcher Kevin Brain has called for a three-pronged approach to tackle the new strategies employed by drinks manufacturers:

■ Tighter regulation of the alcohol industry

■ Educational programmes which recognise that the youth markets for illicit drugs and alcohol have merged

■ Policies to tackle social exclusion. ■

A selection of approved alcopops.

Please, Sir, I'll have a Pint

A meeting about alcohol education chaired by Anne Widdecombe was told that alcoholic drink should be served under controlled conditions in schools in a radical shake-up of health education.

Ms Janet Street-Porter, a broadcaster and newspaper editor, gave the speech as part of a series hosted by the Portman Group, the drinks industry association.

'Banning the sale of alcohol to the under-18s hasn't worked,' Ms Street-Porter points out. 'Why drive young people onto waste land and into their friends' bedrooms to drink furtively? It's just not a recipe for creating a balanced view about drinking in later life.'

Instead, she proposes making alcohol education part of the National Curriculum, and creating low-alcohol rooms in pubs and bars for 16-18-year-olds. It should be separated from the current trend of lumping together illegal substance and alcohol studies, and taught as an issue in its own right. She also suggested that National Lottery funding should provide the bulk of the financial support and criticised the use of so-called role models for anti-drinking campaigns. She said: 'Ginger Spice and David Beckham might be able to flog crisps or hair gel, but I submit that they couldn't get one teenager to drink less.' ■

TEACHERS FEEL INADEQUATE

A new poll today revealed that Britain's teachers feel inadequately prepared to teach pupils about issues surrounding alcohol. The report, presented at a conference on alcohol education, highlights some startling facts:

■ Three-quarters of teachers polled felt they did not have enough training to teach alcohol education.

■ Only 1 to 5 hours of alcohol education were provided throughout a pupil's entire school career.

■ Just 1% of schools that responded to the poll provided lessons on alcohol issues every year.

A sense of humour helps in the serious business of alcohol education.

■ Over half felt that the current levels of alcohol education were totally insufficient.

A recent MORI survey also supports calls for further investment in alcohol education in schools. 65% of those questioned thought schools would provide the best information on sensible drinking. Adults, though, also require more information on issues surrounding alcohol. In the same survey only 28% felt well informed about the risks associated with alcohol. This is despite a significant rise in the number of people who understand what is meant by an 'alcohol unit'. ■

Is Booze Bad for Business?

Is it time to count the financial cost of alcohol abuse?

Drinkers may feel a hangover is an acceptable price to pay for a good night out, but the cost is rather higher for employers. We can begin to see the size of the problem facing the business economy when we consider that drinkers take four times as many days off work as non-drinkers – a staggering 12 million working days are lost each year as a result – and that one in five accidents in the workplace are drink-related.

Alcohol Concern estimates that the cost in lost days and shortened working lives runs at approximately £2.8 billion per year. People suffering from alcohol dependency are more likely to experience problems staying employed. Good attendance, health and punctuality are all essential requirements in any job, but are seldom experienced by problem drinkers.

This is supported by findings in the same report in which Alcohol Concern found that problem drinking affects an individual's ability to work productively. A census of alcohol services found that, of the 10,000 people receiving help for their drinking problems each day, 36% were unemployed.

UNEMPLOYABLE?

Of particular concern is the 16-18-year-old range. 13% of non-participants in employment or education are misusing alcohol.

The French government has recently commissioned Professor Pierre Kopp of the Sorbonne University in an attempt to find out the exact costs of problem drinking. Including tobacco and illicit drugs in the figures, Prof. Kopp concluded that the French economy suffered to the tune of £21 billion per year. More than half that cost was attributable to alcohol.

As well as separating figures for legal and illegal drugs, Kopp also reported that the cost of alcohol may be 'far higher than our figures show because they do not include crime and accidents, theft, rape, domestic violence, attempted suicide' and other marginal costs related to alcohol abuse. ■

GOOD NEWS FOR REAL BREWS

Consumer groups anxious about the recent round of mergers in the drinks industry had good news from the UK's regional brewers in 2000.

Despite Scottish & Newcastle's takeover of Kronenbourg, and the attempted takeover of Whitbread and Bass by the huge Belgian company Interbrew, regional brewers reported strong growth.

Turnover at Young's of Wandsworth was up 10%, Fuller's by 11%, George Gale's by 8%, and Jennings Brothers' draught beers division up by 11%.

Hampshire-based George Gale tempered the good news with a plea to politicians. As its Managing Director Nigel Atkinson points out, the future is made less certain with rising taxes.

This view is supported by Paul Roberts, national officer of the Amalgamated Engineers & Electricians Union. He finds the discrepancy between beer duty here and in mainland Europe absurd. 'Bootleggers are making about 8p a pint profit on their illegal activities. A 2p cut in duty would cut their profit margins by 25%, to the point where the risk of prosecution would not justify the rewards.' ■

Is it time for real brewers to roll out the barrel?

Loading up with cheap beer. Of course, it's all for personal consumption!

HM Customs Hits Booze Cruisers

A newsagent in Yorkshire was the first to feel the full force of a recent crackdown on smuggled alcohol. Mr C. S. Warrtig was jailed for 4 months at Barnsley Magistrates Court after pleading guilty to excise evasion totalling £8,500.

Mike Wells, head of Customs Tax Fraud Division, said after the passing of the sentence: 'Smuggling is not a game.' Figures released for a two-month period after the employment of the new measures show that alcohol goods totalling £395,881 were seized at ports in southern England.

However, even in the light of the maximum 7-year prison sentence, many 'jack-the-lads' seem undaunted. With the abolition of Duty Free between European Union countries in 1999, many more 'booze cruisers' have seen this as an opportunity to cash in. They travel across the Channel for the day and load up with cheap alcohol, seeking to avoid what are seen by many as excessive UK alcohol duties.

A COSTLY CRIME

By law, shoppers can only bring back what can be reasonably consumed by one person – a regulation that the government's new action seeks to enforce. Paymaster General Dawn Primarolo, in her justification of this aim, said: 'This is not a victimless crime; honest shopkeepers are being undercut by these criminals. Currently we lose about £215 million in alcohol taxes. This money could substantially increase funding to our schools and hospitals.'

This is all in theory, of course, and makes us all a victim of booze cruisers. But shouldn't more attention be paid to the professional criminals who make a living from smuggling, rather than the once-a-month day-trippers? For Dawn Primarolo there is no distinction between the two: 'If you cannot satisfy Customs Officers that the goods are for personal use, they will be seized, and a wide range of sanctions may follow.' Perhaps, though, if taxes were not so high, people would be less inclined to participate in smuggling in the first place. ■

WORKING WOMEN DRINK MORE

A recent article by the Institute of Alcohol Studies suggests that 20 per cent of women in the 16-24 age group are drinking more than 14 units per week, compared with 11 per cent in the late 1980s. The heaviest drinkers are likely to be unmarried professionals with higher education degrees and no children.

DRAMATIC CHANGE

Evidence indicates that this trend is largely due to the increase in wages for female professionals, which for some years have lagged behind male employees of an equal grade. There has also been a dramatic change in the attitude towards women who drink. Socially it is more acceptable for women to be seen in a bar, either alone or with friends, and for them to get drunk.

The image of alcohol in the media has also changed as businesses pick up on the potential of the female market. No longer confined to a secret drink at home, alcohol is portrayed as fashionable and glamorous, used by women who are independent, fun-loving and desirable. ■

WHY DO PEOPLE INFLICT A MORNING OF MISERY ON THEMSELVES? FIND ONE ANSWER ON PAGE 25.

PAM DUNSFORD – A VINTAGE CAREER IN AUSTRALIAN WINE

Australian wine is an astonishing success story. But just thirty years ago it was a different matter. Wines from the 'New World', i.e. those not from Europe, were rare and for good reason – they tended to taste awful!

Now though, Australia is a leading producer of premium wine, shipping it world-wide by the tanker-load. Pam Dunsford, busy consultant, highly respected winemaker and successful businesswoman, has certainly contributed more than most to her nation's wine production success.

Pam Dunsford graduated with an Agricultural Science degree at Adelaide University in 1972, majoring in Horticulture and Biochemistry. However, in an interview with Paul Clancy she says: 'I learnt more about winemaking from subsequent mentors when I joined the industry.' Later, Pam did decide to study again, and in 1978 she went to the University of California to take a Masters degree in Food Science.

ALWAYS LEARNING

Pam is always learning, innovating, and bringing the best of modern science to the winemaking process. She is not shy of traditional 'peasant' techniques though, as she recalls from one trip to France: 'The French have been doing it very well for years. For them the entire winemaking process is a matter of style.' Pam discovered one 'should never underestimate the basics – the proven, long established methods'.

Pam now implements her own style at the Chapel Hill winery, sold in 2000 by family-run Gerard Industries to Swiss company Permafix AG. This company already owns Californian winery Cuvaison and vineyards in Argentina and Switzerland. Pam oversees about 700 tonnes of grapes through the wine-making process each year at Chapel Hill. Situated in the McLaren Vale, South Australia, the winery benefits from the local climate. Where some vines struggle to adjust to Australia's searing heat at the height of summer, the Vale is cooled by evening breezes from the nearby sea. The soil is good, and diseases on the vines are almost unheard of. But growing grapes is not Pam's only challenge.

A NEW CHALLENGE

Her blend of experience, tough personality and scrupulous attention to detail have seen her through many problems over the years. But perhaps the most recent one is set to be the toughest: namely the Australian government's dramatic increase on alcohol taxes. Australian winemakers, including Pam Dunsford, have criticised this move, which could cripple premium Australian wine production. They highlight that while these taxes (46%) apply to the entire industry, an additional Value Added Tax also applies to the super premium and ultra premium wine sectors. As these sectors are made up of mostly small to medium-sized wineries, it makes them the most highly taxed, per unit of production, in the world. The future of small scale wine production remains an uncertain one and it's not a problem that even someone with Pam's experience will find easy to solve. ■

Pam Dunsford has helped to make Australian wine a market leader.

Editorial

BRITAIN'S BINGE DRINKING BLUES

The government has acknowledged that Britain has 'a social and cultural problem' with alcohol and its antisocial side-effects. Britain is not the biggest alcohol consumer in the Western world, by far. But it seems that alcohol's place in society is quite different in Britain, even when compared with the habits of our continental cousins. In France, for example, alcohol is incorporated into the daily routine. This usually takes the form of a glass or two with a meal, whereas in Britain, alcohol is used by its main consumers as a means to get 'plastered'.

Binge-drinking is a growing concern. And men are not the only guilty party – women are drinking to excess twice as much as they were a decade ago. Young people are poisoning themselves and choking to death on their own vomit as a result of alcohol at an ever-increasing rate.

Poverty and social exclusion may be one source of the problem. But it's not the whole story – just think of William Hague's brash claims to a 14-pint-a-day youth, or Euan Blair, Tony Blair's son, being scraped from the gutter by the Metropolitan Police at 16 years of age.

How are we to change this 'lager lout' mentality? Easing licensing laws certainly seems an odd way to go about it at first glance, but the continental example should be noted. Instead of forcing revellers to gulp down their last drop at a particular time each evening, we should allow licensed premises to stay open through the night. Drinkers could take their time and go home peacefully.

Ms Street-Porter's suggestion that we introduce young people to alcohol earlier and supervise their first experiences of the drug is perhaps too radical for the current mood. But unless we are prepared to consider ways of restructuring our national culture there can be no end to the 'British disease'. ■

Letters

Peer pressure

I wish someone had taught me a bit more about alcohol when I was a teenager. Just learning how to say no to a drink would have been a start. But everyone drank, didn't they? Your parents, their friends, your friends. Only wimps said no and I didn't want to be one of them. I didn't even like alcohol but I still drank it.

Twenty years later I've learnt to say no – the hard way – courtesy of Alcoholics Anonymous. People may sneer at alcohol 'education' but I for one think it could make a difference.

Yours, Ivor Problem

Tough talk

It seems to me that the world has gone mad! Introducing children to alcohol indeed! The best way to stop under-age drinking is to make sure they cannot get hold of it in the first place. Introduce new laws to crack down on alcohol sales and send those caught drinking to special centres were they can dry out. If these children want to drink like adults, then they should be punished like them too.

Yours, Phil Prisons

Capital crime

I don't do illegal drugs, I don't steal and I've never committed murder. Yet I can't help feeling like a criminal. If I have committed a crime it is only that I enjoy drinking. It's part of my social life. Of course there are times when I have a bit too much, but that's up to me. I'm not an alcoholic, because if that were true, then so are half my office.

Then why do I feel like I'm branded as one by some parts of the press?

Yours, I. M. Okai

Organ outrage

First smokers and now sufferers of alcohol addiction are being passed over for transplant treatments on the unspoken basis that their diseases are 'self-inflicted'.

A four-year study in Montpellier, France, has finally proved that alcoholics with the liver disease cirrhosis are as likely to benefit from a liver transplant as non-drinkers with liver disease.

Will the NHS now come clean and admit that its only reason to deny addicts proper treatment is an outmoded 'pull yourself together' attitude towards victims of addiction?

Yours, Eva Hart

Let's discuss this

Tia Towtell
Alcohol Awareness Campaigner

versus

Ivana Margharita
Drinks Correspondent, The Wallbanger Journal

Alcohol rots our livers, shortens lives, causes fatal accidents, poisons our children, results in teenage pregnancy, encourages domestic violence and public disorder, leads to criminal activities, places burdens on our health service, and costs our economy untold billions of pounds each year.

For this disastrous price, we enjoy what? A few hours of foolish behaviour conveniently forgotten the next day – if we're lucky – and the delights of the painful hangover.

We should grow up and just say 'no'.

Yours
TT

Drinking alcohol allows us to unwind. The comfort of alcohol's warm glow in our bellies encourages us to socialise, to laugh, and even to be more passionate.

Alcohol is an integral part of humanity's development, dating back at least as far as the written word. Its effects permit us to step out of our sober, rule-laden concerns into a world of playfulness. We are permitted to be silly, if only for a short time.

For these reasons, alcohol is of great benefit to society. Without it, life would be just one never-ending hangover.

Yours
IM

It's all very romantic to talk of laughter and passion as a result of alcohol. But what about being capable of taking vital decisions?

What good is passion to a 15-year-old girl once she wakes up to find herself with an unwanted pregnancy? Where will the laughter come from when the policeman tells a father that his child has been killed by a drunk driver?

If you want to know what life as a 'never-ending hangover' would be like, talk to them.

Yours
TT

As ever, the killjoy argument relies on the idea that other people, for whatever reason, are not to be thought of as responsible.

Your 15-year-old girl is, clearly, too inexperienced to handle herself with drink. Your drunken driver is somehow a fact of life, not a person who decided to become drunk and put others' lives at risk.

Look again at your earlier 'price list'. Alcohol no more *causes* those things than God does – it's us humans who raise the glass to our lips.

Yours
IM

I don't think 'killjoy' is an appropriate term to throw at someone tackling alcohol abuse, one of our society's major causes of misery.

If people were responsible, as you claim, how could they avoid knowing that drink driving kills?

How could they fail to understand that alcohol is a toxin which places deadly strains on their health?

The evidence of ages is staring you in the face. People often drink precisely because they want to escape their responsibilities. They need telling, and telling often, that alcohol is no solution.

Yours
TT

The vast majority of people DO know that drink driving kills, and that excessive drinking is bad for the health. We avoid both.

A minority, however, express their immaturity or low self-esteem through alcohol abuse.

Did alcohol *cause* their personality problems in the first place? No. Would they be miraculously cured if we took away this plaything? No.

You seem eager to make millions of responsible drinkers feel guilty for their bit of fun, while making no difference to the real problem – the sad minority.

Yours
IM

THE HARD SELL

Alcohol advertising is a tricky business. Governments know that they can't completely ban it – after all, drinks are legal. Not only that, they are big business and raise lots of tax for governments and consumers expect to be informed of their choices.

On the other hand, how is it possible to put a positive spin on a poison associated with ill-health, violence and countless accidents?

Advertising guidelines are set by law, or by industry agreement. In most countries they demand that advertisements are not misleading; adverts suggesting that drinking alcohol makes you a better, wealthier or more popular person would not be acceptable. Guidelines also require that adverts do not encourage children to drink. Images that appeal to children are discouraged.

But while these seem sensible and fair, it is hard to know where to draw the line. Just by being funny, an advert can give a drink street-credibility (see panel). And there is a less regulated aspect of advertising which worries those campaigning against alcohol abuse.

Modern media are driven by advertising revenue. A magazine or TV programme typically stays in business by 'delivering' an audience to someone who is selling a product. The cover price of a newspaper, for example, represents barely a quarter of the total income the newspaper receives; the rest comes from the advertisers.

SPIN THE BOTTLE

If a TV channel or a magazine carries several stories about the dangers of alcohol, for example, drinks advertisers understandably take their business elsewhere – they do not want an image of their precious bottle to appear next to the headline Alcohol Kills.

This leads to a situation where media that ignore alcohol's bad effects can expect to win advertising from drinks companies away from their more balanced competitors. Two major research studies in the 1980s showed a direct link between the quantity of alcohol adverts and the lack of articles critical of alcohol in magazines.

Such situations are impossible to regulate without massive state intervention. The final judge, in the end, has to be the consumer. ■

This advertisement from the 1930s would not be permitted today.

FAVOURITE ADVERTS

■ 'My favourite advert featured the Budweiser frogs. It had a great story line, including Louis the Iguana.' ADRIAN, 17

■ 'The Guinness advertisement of the surfers was easily the best one ever, a magical work of art. The use of computer manipulation was particularly successful.' RACHEL, 15

■ 'I like the Fosters adverts, they are always so funny!' AMJAD, 13

Will fictional television pubs give way to trendy winebars?

CHANGE OF ART

The Irish brewery Guinness has changed its advertising strategy after studies it commissioned showed that sexy women put men off their pints. Dr Aric Sigman, a psychologist, found that men are less relaxed, and thus less likely to drink heavily, in the presence of a highly attractive woman. But, as publicans point out, sexy barmaids have always been great for improving customer loyalty. ■

Soap Pubs in Peril

Everyone loves a good soap opera, and never more so than when a big knees-up is planned at the local pub. As the regular cast become tired and emotional under the influence, you can be sure that a major drama is about to unfold.

But is the poor old soap pub heading for the scrap heap? Back in the 1980s it seemed that the Queen Vic (EastEnders) might lose its business to an upstart winebar, but the Walford faithful soon saw off the yuppie threat.

Through fires, divorce, attempted murders and assorted adulterous affairs, the Queen Vic has always managed to come out on top.

The Rovers Return (Coronation Street) has also had its fair share of drama. Made famous by feisty barmaid Bet Lynch, who once had to be carried from the pub's blazing shell, it also provided the ring for a right-royal boxing match between Mikc Baldwin and Ken Barlow.

THE BOOZY NEWT

Similar sagas have unfolded in The Woolpack (Emmerdale), The Bull (Archers, the radio soap), and The Dog in The Pond (Hollyoaks).

The nation reacted in horror in November 2000 when it was discovered the Rovers might be sold to a 'soul-less' chain of pubs and renamed The Boozy Newt. It's a name one might expect to grace some pompous middle class drinkerie in a leafy corner of South London, circa 1990.

But there is another more serious threat to soap pubs: alcohol-campaigners are calling attention to the bad example set by soap operas, which show people drinking heavily, even during the day.

Lis Hill, a Scottish health campaigner, argues that Coronation Street sends 'subliminal messages' to workers encouraging them to drink during their lunch breaks. Factory girls imitating the soap's own workers, who invariably pile into the Rovers (or the Newt?) for a liquid lunch, may be endangering their lives by getting drunk before returning to work and operating dangerous machinery.

Mrs Hill raised the alarm because the soap affects people's standards: 'Because it happens all the time in the soap, rather than as a one-off story, it becomes an accepted norm.'

Mrs Hill's argument may not wash with many, though. Given that no one watches telly in soapland, if viewers truly imitated soap characters' behaviour, they'd all switch off their TVs! ■

Oliver Reed, actor and 'hellraiser', went out in style.

Obituary:
Oliver Reed 1938-1999

Actor Oliver Reed was born in Wimbledon, London, on 13th February, 1938, and died on Sunday afternoon, 2nd May, 1999.

Reed was a troublesome youth, running away from home and becoming a bouncer at a Soho stripjoint. Despite a lack of any formal training, he rose to stardom as an actor in the 1960s and 70s. His roles, including Bill Sykes in *Oliver*, and *Women In Love,* where he wrestled in the nude, earned him a fond place in the cinema-going public's heart.

Reed was almost as famous for his extreme appetite for alcohol and the resulting drunken escapades. His appearance always livened up a TV chat show. 'I give them the very thing they want, and sometimes I go over the top,' he once explained. His going over the top, aged 53, on a live Channel 4 programme prompted the Broadcasting Standards Council to issue extra guidelines to programme makers.

Reed was an unapologetic drinker. 'I like the effect drink has on me. What's the point of staying sober?'

He fell ill in a pub on the island of Malta, one Sunday afternoon, during a break in the filming of *Gladiator*. He was rushed to hospital, but died in the ambulance. He was 61 years old.

Actress turned politician Glenda Jackson said, 'I am very sorry he has gone, but I think he probably went the way he would have wished.'

He is survived by his wife, Josephine, and two children by previous partners. ∎

Not That Innocent

One of the world's most famous pop starlets has been drawing a line under her childhood with some quite adult antics involving alcohol.

Britney Spears, a former child star, has spent a few years finding her own feet after being presented to the world as a squeaky-clean teen role model. She has been spotted quite happily 'under the influence' and it is even said to be the reason for her brief marriage.

But she denies that her behaviour is a problem at all. Apart from the natural process of growing up and trying out new experiences, Spears has explained to Associated Press that she has had enough of being told what to do by her elders. "I don't listen to that many people, I'm a very stubborn person. When someone tells me not to do something, I do it, that's just my rebellious nature."

Spears' long-suffering mum Lynne may have some words to say about that! ∎

Completely Unafflected

Tired of hearing about this or that poor little rich celeb checking into rehab because they can't handle how fun their life is? Well, here's a new spin. Actor and screenwriter Ben Affleck has taken himself along to the classy West Coast clinic Promises ... before his drinking gets out of hand!

The heartthrob had some experience of alcoholism as a kid - his parents separated when he was a teenager, largely due to his father's drink problem.

According to his press handler, Affleck was not admitting to anything as serious as alcoholism - he just wanted some tips about keeping it all under control. ∎

Ben Affleck learning by his father's mistakes .

Why Do We Drink?

Alcohol is a toxin excreted by yeasts. Even in small quantities, its presence in the body deadens the reflexes, upsets the kidneys, distracts the liver, and causes chemical upset in almost the entire body. In large quantities, it kills us. So why do we voluntarily pour it down our throats?

The short answer – for pleasure. But pleasure is one of those tricky things philosophers like to write large, confusing books about. Why should a poison amuse us? Are we all suicidal? Or is there a more straightforward reason for enjoying the experience of mild alcohol poisoning?

The brain is one place to look for a culprit. Brains originated as small computers which helped animals locate useful food by sampling molecules in the air – smell machines.

The human brain has developed since then, but smells are still important. Long after words and images have disappeared from your memory, a smell can trigger a vivid flashback of an experience.

Fine, you may say, but hello? What's this got to do with drinking alcohol? Well, alcohol just happens to be one of nature's great smell-makers. Here's the science bit: relatively odourless itself, alcohol is very good at loosening the bonds between molecules and carrying them

This young lady prefers beer to tea: but why?

into the air as it evaporates (this is why most perfumes are alcohol-based). Once the molecules are airborne, we can smell them!

SMELL MACHINES

That's only a part of the story, though. Much experience of alcohol is cultural, as studies of different groups have shown: your reaction to it, beyond basic biological processes, is a learned behaviour.

Alcohol is typically consumed in Western societies whenever people wish to relax and be friendly. As you grow up in such a society, you come to associate alcohol with happiness, warmth and sociability. By the time you are overcoming alcohol's revolting taste (your body still knows it's a poison), the smell may be enough to remind you to relax, to lighten your mood.

It's also at this point, though, that the real danger of alcohol begins. Some people prefer to ignore the causes of stress by hiding them with 'bottled' happiness, resulting in alcohol dependency.

So, we drink for pleasure, and it, in return, gives us pleasure because it tickles our senses and brings happiness to mind. But, couldn't tea do just the same thing? Well it does, doesn't it? Just ask your granny! ■

PUB TALK

■ I envy people who drink – at least they know what to blame everything on.
Oscar Levant, composer, musician and actor

■ Work is the curse of the drinking class.
Oscar Wilde, playright

■ The problem with some people is that when they aren't drunk, they're sober.
W. B. Yeats, poet and author

■ No drug, not even alcohol, causes the fundamental ills of society. If we're looking for the source of our troubles, we shouldn't test people for drugs, we should test them for stupidity, ignorance, greed and love of power.
P. J. O'Rourke, political commentator

■ I'm glad I've given up drugs and alcohol. It would be awful to be like Keith Richards.
Elton John, composer and musician

■ Gosh, drink is sure a filthy thing, isn't it? I'd rather be dead than unable to trust my own eyes!
Robin (in *Batman*, the original series, 1966)

IS DRINKING ALCOHOL A QUESTION OF FAITH?

Religion Editor

Is alcohol really evil? **Well, given that Jesus turned water to wine,** and that most of our modern drinks were developed by generations of monks through the Middle Ages, perhaps Christians should believe the very opposite. But many Christians are very concerned by the social effects of alcohol abuse.

PROHIBITION

In the early 20th century, a Christian-inspired 'temperance' movement succeeded in banning alcohol in the USA. The ban, known as Prohibition, did not work. The practice of socialising over a glass of wine, beer or spirits was so deeply ingrained it proved impossible to police. Prohibition's only significant effect was to allow petty criminals to earn a fortune and become organised into mafia-style syndicates commanding huge wealth.

In any case, one common

Communion.

theme for Christians is the Eucharist – the wine and bread consumed in a religious service known as Holy Communion. With the exception of Quakers and the Salvation Army, all Christians may take part in this ceremony, where the bread and wine symbolise the body and blood of Christ.

Some Christians believe that the blessing of a priest or minister turns the wine and bread into the *actual* blood and flesh of Christ, and they honestly claim never to touch wine. But for most, the ritual is a symbolic act of sharing in a Christian fellowship born out of Christ's self-sacrifice.

Wine is simply part of religious practice.

Muslims take a far stronger stand on the subject: all alcohol is ungodly – and most observe total abstinence from alcohol. Along with other mind-altering drugs, alcohol is specifically forbidden to followers by the Qu'ran.

DIVINE KNOWLEDGE

True, certain branches of Islam – Sufism, in particular – associate wine with aspects of divine knowledge. The Qu'ran itself colours its description of the landscape of Paradise with rivers of wine. But these are sacraments no mortal Muslim should expect to lay hands on in this world; the positive associations granted to wine are Allah's gift to those who have lived worthy lives.

Though Islam tolerates non-believers having a drink, in countries that are ruled under Islamic law – shar'ia – alcohol is illegal. Iran and Saudi Arabia are the two main Islamic countries to be run according to the shar'ia. It is also observed in several other smaller countries in the Middle East, including most of the Gulf States and Afghanistan. Unlike Christian cultures, this prohibition is relatively easy to enforce as it coincides with the people's existing social practices.

However, partly because Islam is a way of life, followers in different countries take the laws more or less literally. (In the same way, Christians interpret the stories of the Bible according to the particular church they follow.) In practice, this means that in some Muslim states alcohol is fairly easily obtainable.

SPIRITUAL CODE

Sikhism is another religion where alcohol is forbidden, although the religion is flexible enough to tolerate many interpretations.

A common theme for all the major religions emerges. In theory, they say, alcohol is not good for you. It is a case of personal choice – as our witnesses show. A little bit now and again, in the right social context, won't send you to Hell. It might require some apologising to your community afterwards. But excess drinking, and drinking as a way of life, are things to be avoided. The common sense shared by all religions, it turns out, is moderation. ■

W I T N E S S :
Norman Clayton is a practising Methodist. But the fact that he is a non-drinker pre-dates his Methodism. In a society where drinking alcohol is a socially accepted way of life, Norman has made a lifestyle decision.
'It's not even something I think about. I don't drink, and I never have done.
'People are always trying to find out why I don't drink, as if something was wrong with me! It makes me laugh, especially when people ask, "Well, you don't drink, but do you drink Champagne?" I am heavily involved with my church, not only on Sundays! Methodism has a fairly open mind about alcohol. I know quite a few of our congregation "like a drink".
'Of course I visit pubs for meals. My friends know I won't have a pint, or any alcohol. I think of it in the same way that some people don't drink coffee or tea, and they don't get given a hard time!
'I do think about my health, but even that is not a reason

Norman Clayton made a lifestyle decision not to drink.

for not drinking. It's something I've never done, and never will do.' ■

W I T N E S S :
Bindi Singh Sohi, Publican at The Orange Peel Public House, Hillingdon, North London.
'Some people in the Sikh community think I'm selling out a bit, but I'm earning a good, honest living and most people respect that.

'My faith offers me general guidelines, and it's up to me how I interpret the scriptures on drinking. I choose not to drink. Sikhism allows me to follow my own path.
'I love being behind the bar. It's a really relaxed and social environment to work in. We do get the odd customer who goes a bit over the top. You certainly see the ups and downs of drinking on this job.' ■

Cultural reactions to alcohol

Attitudes to alcohol vary hugely with culture and faith. Its use is much more widespread and 'normal' in 'Western' cultures. Alcoholism, too, is rare beyond these 'Western' cultures, even where alcohol is regularly used. The patterns of behaviour associated with alcohol intoxication are quite different to the extent that many cultures do not even recognise hangovers as an after-effect of alcohol use.

The Quecha people of Peru pursue drunkenness as part of their cultural practices, and yet do not experience hangovers. Similar immunity to alcohol's after-effects has been recorded among certain Polynesian groups.

That said, some cultures who have only been introduced to alcohol by European settlers have not shown such tolerance. In North America in the 17th century, the Iroquois Indians of New York State and south-eastern Canada incorporated

European alcohol into existing religious ceremonies. However they banned it a few decades later when drunkenness got out of hand.

In the 19th century, the Aboriginal population of Australia was ravaged by European introduced diseases to which they had no resistance. Their reaction to alcohol, also something they had never met, was equally disastrous and problems with alcohol abuse within their community continue today. ■

England Fans in Beer Experiment

The Sports Editor

Violence between rival fans in Copenhagen prompted Dutch authorities to take an unusual step for the Euro 2000 tournament.

British club Arsenal met Turkish club Galatasaray in the Danish city for the Uefa Cup final, but the event was overshadowed by a series of violent confrontations between rival fans, including several stabbings.

As Belgian and Dutch police prepared for further lawlessness during the Euro games, hosted jointly by the two countries, the city of Eindhoven struck upon a unique plan.

The city council ordered thousands of gallons of half strength beer, banning sales of full strength alcoholic drinks from the town during the games. Result? The Dutch town enjoyed a friendly, carnival atmosphere.

Kevin Miles, representing the English Football Supporters' Association in Eindhoven, was keen to point out that most fans are not hooligans. 'They were playing football with the police joining in. It's been fantastic.'

Low-alcohol beer helped maintain the 'carnival' mood throughout the day.

Dr Rein Welschen, Eindhoven's mayor, noted that 'This is good for England and it was great for Eindhoven.'

FANS AREN'T YOBS

Alcohol has long been identified with the problem of football hooliganism, particularly in relation to British clubs. Drink-fuelled violence is now commonly referred to as 'the British disease' in continental football circles. Sadly, the example of Eindhoven was swiftly forgotten in the Euro games when violence once again erupted in Belgium.

Home Secretary Jack Straw observed that: 'There's a social and cultural problem in this country to do with alcohol-related violence.' His department rushed through new legislation after further rioting by British 'fans' – which had resulted in almost 800 being deported by Belgian authorities. In Brussels, Mayor de Donnea found the behaviour of England fans 'disgusting'. ■

France Blocks Deal

A French law known as the 'Loi Evin' prevented American beer giant Budweiser, sponsor of the World Cup 1998, placing advertisements within participating stadiums. The Loi Evin bans alcohol and tobacco advertising on TV, and stadium posters would have been visible to television viewers. ■

EX-ADDICT GIVES HOPE

Former Arsenal captain Tony Adams has announced plans to launch a clinic to treat footballers with alcohol problems.

Adams, whose own battle with alcoholism has left him drink-free since 1996, wants to open a 12-bed centre dedicated to the particular needs of celebrity sportsmen and women.

Coping with the fame and media attention that comes with world-class football can be hard for young players. The Football Association is well aware of the problem, and says it is assisting Adams in every way it can. ■

Mr Adams earned praise for his autobiography describing his alcohol dependence.

SPONSORSHIP AND SPORT

The government has rejected calls to limit the alcohol industry's contribution to sports sponsorship.

The calls have been headed by the British Medical Association, which in a recent report of its own found a need for greater control. A similar move led to restrictions on tobacco sponsorship, worth around £10 million a year. However, Prime Minister Tony Blair has refused to back the BMA. In a meeting with sports administrators he said: 'There is no such thing as a safe cigarette but there is a reasonable balance that can be struck when drinking alcohol.'

Alcohol sponsorship in Britain is believed to be worth around £100 million a year. The bulk of this is made up by leading sports which include:

■ Football – FA Carling Premier League (£36 million 4-year deal)
■ Rugby – Heineken Cup (approximately £800,000 per year)
■ Tennis – Stella Artois tournament (between £700,000 and £1 million per year)

ENCOURAGED TO DRINK

It certainly seems as though the link between sponsorship and its subsequent 'effects' is a tenuous one at best. However, pressure groups continue to insist that youngsters, in particular, are being engineered to associate sport with alcohol.

MAKING BOOZE SEXY

More suprisingly, Lee Lixenberg of Alcohol Concern feels it is certainly 'encouraging them to drink more'. He goes on to say: 'The whole issue of youngsters wearing football replica shirts (e.g. Liverpool's Carlsberg logo) concerns us. Many are nothing short of walking advertising boards for the drinks companies. The danger is that alcohol is seen as exciting and sexy.'

But just because a logo appears on a sports shirt, it cannot be assumed that it will have an 'effect' on those wearing it. Telecommunication, insurance and even double-glazing companies sponsor sports, but they are not perceived as exciting or sexy. It is the multi-million pound sports world itself, dominated by high-class athletes, that appeals more to youngsters. And these athletes know, more than anyone, that getting drunk is not the way to guarantee a five-figure pay packet at the end of each week! ■

WHO'S WHO

Here are just some of the groups committed to the promotion of alcohol awareness and education. They provide a good starting point for further study, including links and addresses to many other organisations.

UNITED KINGDOM

■ **Alcohol & Alcoholism Journal**
Fascinating reports of recent laboratory research
www.alcalc.oupjournals.org

■ **Alcohol Concern**
Campaign group news and archives.
Waterbridge House, 32-36 Loman Street, London SE1 0EE
www.alcoholconcern.org.uk

■ **Campaign for Real Ales**
Beer-lovers' consumer group, promoting diversity and traditional beer-making techniques, campaigning for wider consumer choice and conser-vation of Britain's pub heritage. 230 Hatfield Road, St Albans, Herts AL1 4LW
www.camra.org.uk

■ **Department of Health**
Press releases and some weighty material on new health-related laws in the pipeline (White Papers and Green Papers).
Richmond House, 79 Whitehall, London SW1A 2NS
www.doh.gov.uk

■ **The Portman Group**

Alcohol Education Resource Directory, provided by the drinks industry's self-regulation body. Includes forms for ordering pamphlets and selected free resources. 7-10 Chandos Street, Cavendish Square, London W1G 9DQ
www.portman-group.org.uk

■ **Wine and Spirit Educational Trust**
Provides training courses for consumers and professionals in the fine arts behind wines and spirits. www.wset.co.uk

■ **Wrecked**
A weird little site from the Department of Health most notable for its collection of sad and occasionally revolting drinking tales from teenagers.
www.wrecked.co.uk

AUSTRALIA

■ **Alcohol & Other Drugs Council of Australia**
Supports the government, the media and general community, by providing accessible information. 17 Napier Close, Deakin ACT 2605
www.adca.org.au

■ **Family Drug Support**
A website designed to assist families throughout Australia to deal with drug and alcohol issues in a way that strengthens relationships and achieves positive outcomes.
Hotline: 1300 368 186
www.fds.org.au

■ **National Alcohol Campaign** Provides

information, frequently asked questions and answers, downloadable television commercials and website links on alcohol.
www.nationalalcoholcampaign.health.gov.au

NEW ZEALAND

■ **Alcohol Advisory Council of New Zealand**
Primary objective is to promote moderation in the use of alcohol and to develop strategies that will reduce alcohol related crime. ALAC, Level 13, Castrol House, 36 Customhouse Quay, PO Box 5023, Wellington, NZ
www.alcohol.org.nz

Note to parents and teachers
Every effort has been made by the Publishers to ensure that these websites are suitable for children; that they are of the highest educational value, and that they contain no inappropriate or offensive material. However, because of the nature of the Internet, it is impossible to guarantee that the contents of these sites will not be altered. We strongly advise that Internet access is supervised by a responsible adult.

GO ON, TALK ABOUT IT

The Alcohol News doesn't just want to give you its views on the news. It wants you, its readers, to talk about the issues too. Here are some questions to get you started:

■ Is alcohol advertising more regulated than alcohol consumption?
■ Is there peer pressure to drink? If you think there is, why do you think it happens?

■ Why do most people choose to drink?
■ Do the benefits of alcohol as a stress-reliever outweigh the risks for pregnant women?
■ Can alcohol realistically be banned?
■ Why should taxpayers cover the cost of illness and injury caused by silly drinkers?
■ Is alcohol to blame for accidents, or are the people who got drunk still responsible?

■ Does abstaining from alcohol make people less able to socialise?
■ Are medical risks reason enough to remove people's freedom of choice?
■ Is alcoholism a physical, psychological or social problem, or a mixture of these?
■ Should governments take all our moral choices for us?
■ At what age should people be allowed to buy drink?

WHAT'S WHAT

Here's *The Alcohol News'* quick reference aid explaining some terms you'll have come across in its pages.

■ **addiction** A learned behaviour which makes the sufferer dependent on the consumption of a drug such as alcohol, without which they feel distressed. Chemical addiction describes the bodily processes which cause the sufferer pain if the drug is withheld.

■ **alcohol** Normally meaning ethanol, a hydrocarbon compound excreted by yeasts which has unusual effects on body chemistry, particularly by jamming the normal interaction of nerve cells in the brain. Other alcohols include cholesterol and methanol.

■ **alcopops** Recently-invented drinks slightly stronger than beer, made by adding ethanol to sweetened fruit juices.

■ **anti-depressant** One of various prescription drugs intended to help manage feelings of sadness. Patients are warned not to mix use with alcohol, and to take care when operating machinery or driving.

■ **antioxidants** Chemicals which help prevent oxidation, which can be harmful to the normal functions of cells in the body.

■ **apartheid** The racist political programme of 'separate development', used in South Africa to deny blacks access to white-held social resources and democratic power, confining them to impoverished 'homelands'.

■ **attitude survey** A questionnaire designed to reveal what respondents believe.

■ **blood-alcohol level** The percentage of alcohol found in the bloodstream, normally measured in grams per litre. Alcohol begins to impair body systems at around 0.3 grams per litre, while 4 grams per litre is often fatal.

■ **code of conduct** A set of rules about acceptable behaviour that is decided between people and companies by mutual agreement; rather than a law imposed by democratic vote.

■ **continental** Literally 'belonging to the continent'. In Britain, this refers to the continent of Europe, and is another way to refer to mainland Europe.

■ **Customs** The law enforcement department responsible for border control, particularly ensuring that goods are not smuggled into a country without the appropriate taxes being paid.

■ **dehydration** Serious water loss, due either to excessive urinating and sweating, or to inadequate water intake, which in extreme cases can result in significant brain cell damage.

■ **diversify** Finding new areas of business to add to existing services, normally to safeguard against one market failing - ie, not having 'all your eggs in one basket'.

■ **duty** A type of tax which is paid on goods that are brought across a border from one country to another.

■ **European Commission** A sort of 'board of governors' for the European Union, which is responsible for the daily business of the European Community.

■ **head** The froth that gathers on the surface of certain types of beer as dissolved gases are released during pouring and bubble to the surface.

■ **insulin** A protein hormone produced by the pancreas, vital in controlling blood sugar levels. Sufferers of the disease Diabetes usually require insulin injections to maintain control of their blood sugar levels.

■ **journal** A specialist magazine for scientists and other researchers to share detailed reports of their latest findings.

■ **liver** The organ in the body that cleans and enriches the bloodstream.

■ **liver disease** Overwork caused by alcohol poisoning often leads to cirrhosis of the liver, a disease which gradually replaces functioning tissue with fat and scar tissue, leading to high blood pressure, comas and internal bleeding.

■ **measure** A standard quantity of alcoholic drink sold by the glass. A single measure of a spirit sold in a British public house is 0.03 litres, or one eighteenth of a pint.

■ **methanol** An alcohol related to the ethanol in legal drinks. Humans have few enzymes capable of processing methanol. Those that can are found in quantity in the retina of the eye. In contact with methanol they produce formaldehyde, causing blindness.

■ **moonshine** Spirits illegally distilled without a licence or imported without paying duty.

■ **phenols** Weak acids, particularly abundant in red wine, which in certain circumstances may prevent blood platelets forming clots, so reducing the risk of heart attacks.

■ **pressure group** A voluntary organisation formed to 'put pressure' on politicians to make a specific change - or series of changes - to the law. Pressure groups can call on several experts to back up their side of an argument, but may not be the best source of impartial information.

■ **public house** A licensed building in which alcohol is sold for immediate consumption.

■ **sanctions** Punishments for breaching agreements.

■ **selective breeding** Applying artificial evolutionary pressure to enhance plants or animals under laboratory conditions.

■ **shebeen** An illegal drinking den, where cheap alcohol may be drunk at all times of day or night.

■ **sponsorship** Providing money or other support, normally in return for publicity and marketing opportunities for a specific product or brand name.

■ **test purchasing** Buying something from a shop or supplier in order to research how it is sold, often using a particular customer type (such as a teenager) to do the purchasing.

■ **toxin** A poisonous substance, normally of organic origin.

■ **tribunal** A process similar to a court hearing, by which past conduct is assessed by an independent panel, who make a judgment everyone agrees to follow.

■ **unit** A standard measure used in calculating alcohol intake and its effects.

INDEX